CW00407738

1

Dearest Darling

By

Bilko

Although this book is published in my name,
it is my Wife who is the real author,
and I publish it as a tribute to her.

As my late wife passed away from Sepsis all the proceeds
from this book will go to the Sepsis Trust

With a small thanks to Ed Chandler for his time and help in
putting this book together.

Dearest Darling – Introduction

During one of my sorting out sessions of my late wife's personal possessions, I found in a drawer a bundle of letters that she had written and sent to me back in 1969.

These letters had been written by her whilst I was on 'Exercise' back in West Germany, with 17 Squadron Royal Corps of Transport Workshop REME. The Workshop was then based in Deverill Barracks, Ripon, North Yorkshire, where we had our Married Quarter.

The twenty three letters posted to me cover the period 9th September to 8th November 1969. During the period 3rd to 18th October some letters had gone astray, hence the content of the correspondence. I had obviously saved these letters whilst I was in Germany, and my Wife must have 'reacquired' them on my return to the UK, and she had placed them in a 'safe place' because I never found them until 2019, fifty years later!

Having read some of these letters I have decided to transcribe them to the computer so that you can read of some of the things that she used to write to me about, and it will give you an insight into Service Life at the time, in particular how the absence of the father affected the children emotionally, and the stresses that it placed upon the families.

Whilst typing these handwritten letters to the Computer I have added quotation marks to the speech, and one or two punctuation marks to aid the reader, and allow a more relaxed style in keeping with the sentiment and emotions of these personal letters. All names mentioned have been changed to avoid any embarrassment to the original person.

Our children at this time were aged: Alex 7 years, Ben 5 years, Charlie 4 years, David 3 years and Little Ed 2 years

Bilko

Saturday 6 September
Dearest Darling,

Well I thought I would surprise you and write before you wrote to me. I didn't sleep very well last night and I heard the trucks leaving at three o'clock and had just dropped off to sleep when I woke feeling sick. I had a couple of Disprins but couldn't get back to sleep, so I was up at half past six. The boys had a bath, their hair washed and dressed ready for school at half past seven, the clock was an hour fast. I am fed up already, I kept looking for you at NAAFI break and lunch time, still after a week you get used to it, I hope. I got a lot of work done today and took the boys to the Post Office this afternoon.

We waited for Alex & Ben from school, then came home for tea, we watched television then I took them over to the swings for a while, then got them ready for bed. Little Ed keeps saying "Night, Night Daddy, helicopter", We saw one today and he thinks you have gone in one, still they won't forget you, I have your photograph on the sideboard.

I haven't any more news so I'll leave this letter open until I have more news for you tomorrow, okay,

Darling. I miss you so much Darling, take care of
yourself, we love you very much.
XXXXXXXXXX

Monday 8 September
Dearest Darling,
                    I didn't have very much news before,
so I'll finish this letter tonight. I went down town
Saturday and put the three big boys into the
pictures and wandered round town until three
o'clock, then collected them and we came home on
the bus.
The boys didn't go to Sunday school yesterday, they
all had the cold and are really miserable. I have
had plenty to do so I don't have a lot of time to sit
and think.
I got a letter from my Sister; she might be coming
down in four weeks time to keep me company. Her
husband will hire a car and bring her down and go
back the next day, she isn't quite sure yet as she
doesn't know how she will feel after she has had the
baby, it is due this week. My Dad has got his
problems now, His girlfriend brought her mother
down and she won't bloody budge, he'll never get rid
of her, I know only too well what she is like and her
daughter is having the little girl taken off her, so

she is thinking of taking her in too. My father will have to work like hell to try and keep that lot, it's not fair, what has he ever done to be treated this way, it's really upset me to think he has been lumbered again. They are sending my Auntie home in the next week or so, as they can do no more, so it's only a matter of time now.

The baby budgie is getting really big now, the birds are fine so are the goldfish.

Well that's all my news for now, please write soon Darling. Don't worry about your engine and saving money. I mean, I have put £50 in your Post Office book. Do you want me to send some every week or will I leave it there for you when you come home, let me know in your letter? That's a nice surprise isn't it. Don't be thinking any wrong will you.

The boys miss you so much, so do I Darling. I am thinking of you always. Bye for now. All our love & kisses.

Your loving Wife & sons
XXXXXXXXXXXXX

Saturday 13 September

Dearest Darling,

          I received your welcome letter and pleased to hear from you, I only wish they were a bit longer, I look forward to a long letter.

I miss you very much darling, I wish the ten weeks were up, I do honestly. The boys are really missing you this time, they are off their food. Thursday night I was up most of the night with Charlie, he fell and hurt his ear and there was a horrible discharge coming from it, he is alright now and last night David screamed the house down, he fell asleep at twenty to nine this morning, he has a bad chest, if he is no better tomorrow I'll get the Doctor to him.

The boys been getting up to mischief, I have had four people to the door complaining and one woman said she would give Charlie and David a good belting if they go near her fence again, I just answered the door, didn't say anything, then said "I'll see what the boys say" and closed the door. I don't want any trouble while you're away and I'm certainly not going to give them a hiding for other people. I let them out and go over the play park with them.

We are having a bit of trouble with the Benson children, they have been hitting the boys on the school bus and have been telling them to go to corner shop and steal sweets, or they will bash them. So if there is any more trouble I will go to see the teacher, I have seen Mrs Benson and she said she can't control them while her husband is in Germany, and I said "I can't stop them from playing round our front, if they keep getting our boys into trouble I'll go to the police", I mean it. David and Charlie came home the other night shaking and crying the Benson kids bashed them and said they been pinching from the shop. I went round and found that they hadn't been stealing.

It has been thunderstorms for the last three days and my back has been agony, I seem to be working more now than I did when you were at home.

I will answer your letter now. I am managing the Agencies alright, there was a letter from Wigfalls. I had better enclose it so you can sort it out or I will make a mess of it again. Let me know what to do as soon as you can.

The boys are getting off to school no bother, in fact I am fed up of six o'clock reveille Saturday & Sunday included. The bus leaves at twenty to nine so they leave at twenty past eight so they don't miss it. Last Monday they had to take dinner money, so I had to be there at half eight when the Post Office opened. Last week we just got to the bus stop and the bus went sailing down the road. So it cost me £1 for a taxi to take them to school.

Alex likes the juniors and Ben likes his new teacher, they are always asking about you, the other morning I was sweeping the stairs when the postman pushed your letter through the door. Little Ed was in the kitchen and I said "Oh! a letter from Daddy", so he came charging through "Hello my Daddy" he must have thought it was you at the door, he always sees a helicopter and says "Daddy gone in a helicopter". Ha! Ha! He is a right little terror.

Charlie has been really terrible, not messing himself but keeps wetting the bed. I think I will have to take him to the doctors if he doesn't get any better. David went to the corner yesterday looking for you and wouldn't come home.

Don't let it get you down, you might get your transfer soon, I hope so. Could you send me some overalls over, seeing you have the money for your engine now please.

The baby budgie is getting on fine, he is almost the size of Betty now, he is grey back and head, turquoise and blue tail and a lovely blue breast, he is always hungry, he keeps jumping out of the nesting box, he doesn't like it at all. I speak to him and he snuggles up, he has bitten me a few times. He can't perch properly yet as his tail isn't very long yet, he has a name, I call him Buddy, he looks at me when I say "Hello Buddy Boy".

I see Jane usually every afternoon and we go down to the shops on a Monday and Saturday, but I am on my own every evening. I usually iron and tidy the sitting room up.

I got a card from Mary Knowles, she is getting used to the heat now and the flat isn't as bad as she expected. I am waiting for your reply to my last letter, I hope Monday.

Charlie has just woken up, it's twelve o'clock, he has just wet all over the bed and floor, what a lad he is, lying on the settee grinning like a Cheshire cat. The fish are alright, Jolly is jealous, she got out tonight. I had Buddy on my knee and she came sidling up and started pulling threads out of my shirt. She kept looking at Buddy, as much to say, what are you doing? Buddy started kissing her thinking it was Betty feeding her, and Jolly had a fit, and went flying right round the room, she's a dopey devil.

13

I am managing not too bad with the money so far. I don't have papers now, I will have to start getting coke as it is nearly finished and it is so cold and damp here now. (I miss my hot water bottle), I have put two extra blankets on the bed.

The boys have kept out of the garden, but all the nails came out of the fence where you took the trailer out, and the wind has been blowing it right out there. There's been about three dogs and that flaming cat from along the road messing in the garden. So I chased them, but the new grass is lovely, it's about one inch long and should be nice when it is fully grown.

I posted the birthday cards last week to your Mum and Dad, I went in about the ornament for the garden, they should have some more in a few weeks time, as they are out of stock.

Well I don't suppose I will know it is my Birthday on the sixteenth, it will come and go like any other day. I am going out to see about getting the fence repaired, all the kids in the neighbourhood were lifting the fence and have been breaking pieces off, there will be no fence shortly.

Well my Darling that's all my news for now. We are thinking of you always.

Take care of yourself (don't get too skinny) God Bless.

Your loving Wife and sons.
A Big hug and kisses for Daddy from your fellas.
XXXXX

Budgies 4   Goldfish 2   Ha! Ha!

Sunday 14th September

Dearest Darling,

I am enclosing the letters that Wigfalls sent me, could you tell me how to sort it out please. I will see if Mrs Kay has a permanent address so she can get her own Wigfalls Catalogue Agency, she should know by now.

Well today has passed quickly, I've done a load of washing and housework as Monday is my shopping day, I have nearly ironed all your shirts and have hung them up in your wardrobe. It rained all night, and when I went out this morning with the washing the grass is getting on well, I have been chasing the dogs and cats out or else they will ruin it.
I had a horrible shock tonight Charlie came running up to the front door to tell me something and he tripped and nearly knocked himself out on the steel edge, he got up and put his head on my jumper and he was bleeding like anything, he has a nasty gash on his head, I was shaking like a leaf so Len next door rushed him up to the Medical Room, they put butterfly stitches in, but I will still take him to the Doctors tomorrow, you can't be too careful.

Well I have to be up early in the morning to bath the boys before school. I'll be glad when this ten weeks is over. I am hoping to hear from you tomorrow, if not definitely Tuesday the sixteenth. Darling can you get me some nice ornaments before you come home?

Well that's all my news for now, we miss you very much darling, take care of yourself. Write soon.

All my love Darling, I love you so much, be good. Bye for now, your loving Wife and sons.
XXXXXXXXXX

Monday Night 15 September
Dearest Darling,

       Well I didn't have a letter from you today, still I might hear from you tomorrow. I haven't a lot of news so it will be a short letter.

I got a Birthday card for little Eddie from Mary and Joe, they must have thought tomorrow was his birthday.

I got a Birthday card with a £1 in it so I bought myself two ornaments, they are in John Menzies window, they are gorgeous, two bunny rabbits in beds, all hand painted, they cost 12/11d each.

I have been in the Florists twice about the Heron for your mother's garden, but they said they are having a bit of bother getting one, but they are going to do their best. They won't be getting anymore Messowax in until next summer.

The budgie is getting on fine, I pick him up and he sits on my apron, he isn't scared at all, he has been trying to flutter his wings, he hates the nesting box now, he is having a little nibble of millet spray tonight.

Today has been a queer sort of day. I had a bad night with Charlie, I took him in our bed and he was moaning and groaning half the night.
Jane is fed up, so she is going home on Saturday, so I will be completely lost, I am on my own every night, but she used to keep me company for a while and I always have her to go down town on a Monday, it's fine company.

They took the TV away and gave us a big TV, it was only away for two days and they fixed it, there was something really wrong with it, he said it only cost 6d, but it was a good job it was done.
They still haven't come about the fence, so I will go and see them tomorrow, as it is almost falling to pieces.
Well I haven't much more news Darling, so I will close now, hoping to hear from you tomorrow.

I love you very much and miss you Darling, I am looking forward to seeing you again. The boys are missing you and send their love. Take care of yourself.

Your ever loving Wife and sons.
XXXXXXXXXXXXXXXXXXXXXX

Tuesday 16 September

Dearest Darling,

              Well I received your letter this morning was disappointed as you never sent me a Birthday Card. I thought at least a card. The boys bought me a card and a bag of sweets and were all delighted when they handed them over, they all came trooping into the kitchen with big smiles all over their faces.

Today has been pouring of rain so we haven't been able to get out anywhere. Did you get the boy's letter and pictures yet? They shut the envelope before I could even check it, so I have no idea what they sent you. You'll be even more surprised getting a letter every day, there's not much news from day to day though.

I will answer your letter now.
I am hopeless with being on my own at nights, I have a good old feed up! Not really, but if I get carried away with the film on the TV. I have a munch of chocolate or something.
No! I haven't heard from my sister yet so I have no idea if she is coming down or not, I think she is?

Of course it was my Father who sent me the money, who do you think it was my boyfriend? Don't be so daft. I am managing not too bad with my money. I haven't been broke yet so far. If the boys behave themselves I let them go to the pictures. I take them down for quarter to ten on Saturday morning and collect them at twelve o'clock.

So I just look at the shops until they come out. What can I enjoy, I never have a lot left after the bills are paid, I can tell you.

Would you like a food parcel with some things in? Let me know as soon as you can.

I have sent the Wigfall letter on to you so you should get it soon.

The letter I got this morning took four days to get here. You keep saying write to me soon, I have written every night, I haven't enough news for two letters a day.

I am writing this letter while the boys are still up and as you can see from the writing the noise is terrible, they keep saying "Let me write something", so I'll get them to put a small letter in this one or else they gaily help themselves to my paper, stamps and envelopes. Flaming sauce, I went to get the big writing pad the other day and it had vanished. So I asked Alex where it was, he said "Oh! I drew a few

little pictures". There's dozens of them lying all over the place.
There's been no mail for you. Did you write to Mr Smith about the engine?

Well that's all my news again, we are missing you very much and looking forward to see you soon. Hope to hear from you soon.
Bye for now. God Bless.
All my love...
Your loving Wife.
A big hug and kisses to Daddy from your sons
XXXXXXXXXXXX

Wednesday 17 September

Dearest Darling,

           Well as you probably know by my last letter I was upset because I knew you had bought me a card and I thought you had forgotten to post it. I got your letter telling me where the cards were, still better late than never.

They were lovely especially the one with the roses on, thank you very much.

I will answer Saturday's letter which I received this morning. I can't understand why you haven't got my letters yet, I write to you every night, it's costing me a fortune in stamps, but it's worth it. I think so anyway. It sounds although you have plenty of spare time, lucky devil.

The boys went out to play and the Benson kids got hold of them, threw a big stone at Alex's head, so he came home screaming his head off, he has a lovely bump on his head and is split not deep enough for stitches, yet he had a lovely headache. It's got to stop before there is real trouble, I won't bother going to the door, I had some trouble with her two eldest girls a week ago and she didn't do anything about it.

The budgie is lovely, he has been pecking at the iron block and had a nibble of seed, as soon as it sees its mother he squawks his head off, the noise is terrible, he or she? Is a bit like his father (Bobby) a right little glutton.

The grass is getting on fine if only the dogs would stay out of the garden. They haven't come about the fence, always full of promises but nothing ever done about it.

The boys are always saying "Is daddy coming back soon".

Well darling that's all my news again.
I love you and miss you so much.
Bye for now, God Bless, Love and kisses from us all.
Your loving Wife and sons
XXXXXXXXXXXXXXXXXX

Thursday Night 18 September
Dearest Darling,

I will answer your letter which you wrote on Sunday. Nice and sunny there, it has done nothing but rain the last week, I don't let the three little ones out to play now as I had five people in one day come to the door complaining, and one woman said she'd give them a good hiding if they went near her gate , so I just take them out. Charlie has done nothing but wet his bed twice a night since you left. Little Ed is very 'niggly' just now, he always says "Daddy is gone in boat and helicopter", you should hear him talking to David.
If David hits him he says, "I'm telling Mummy David" and comes crying to me. When he saw the Birthday Cards he kept singing "Happy Birthday to my Mummy". He is a proper little rascal. When I say "Come here or I will smack you" he says "No! You dare! Ha! Ha! He is always saying "Ooh! Ah! Cha! Cha! Cha!" You know where he gets that expression. He knows you have gone and he just accepted it now just like me, they have to or else we would be miserable all the time. Only one more day and the three big boys go to the pictures and I have the morning to myself to wander round looking at the

shops. I will have to buy them all new shoes, I will buy them a pair as soon as I can.

I did take them over the swings but the Benson girls started laughing and shouting dirty things, so I don't bother, I can always take them to Witham Road Play Park, it's terrible to think you can't even let the boys out to play but there's always someone coming to the door complaining. People have it in for me as soon as they go out, you can guarantee there's someone at the door. I just say "Yes" and close the door, they haven't pinched or anything so they haven't even had a smack since you went away. I let them stay up until eight o'clock and there's not a sound in the bedroom, the two little ones go to bed at quarter past six and sleep until half past eight in the morning. It's dark here at quarter past seven in the evening so once the boys are in bed I make myself something to eat, do some ironing and tidy up then I write letters.

I got a letter from my Dad, not much news, my sister still hasn't had the baby by Tuesday, she was hoping to start on my Birthday, she even went to the Bingo Tuesday night, she said "Maybe the excitement of the Bingo would start her off".

I might phone your Mum on Monday night when I've got paid, I'll let you know any news.

I wouldn't mind going into the pictures with the boys but I doubt if David and Eddie would sit still, it's only a shilling each for us all.

I've got a disappointment for you, it is only £45 not £50, I bought the two little ones a new pair of shoes with the £5. Sorry love, but I have put the money in your book so I can't get anymore. My Dad sent it so you can get a engine for the car, he must be having a hell of a time, there's not much he can do, still, it's no use my sister and me interfering it's his life and he will just have to sort it out. I don't know if she is still coming, I think she is, it will be alright to have some company as I am cheesed off talking to myself.

I got a letter from Mary today, she likes Bahrain, she said it isn't so bad as she expected, she is still cleaning the quarter, she has been there three weeks now, she said to send their regards when I wrote to you.

I have had a lot of mail as I have been writing like mad to everyone and especially you, so don't say I haven't written, I have been getting writer's cramp. I'll need to get a load of stamps on Monday as I only have one left.

I hope you get the Wigfall letter sorted out or that will be something else to sort out.

I don't know what's wrong with Charlie, David and Ed, they have a cooked meal as usual and a pudding but they have just been 'picking'. This morning when I woke up it was pouring of rain again, that's more than a week of rain and at night and there's that horrible cold damp mist.

I am managing quite well with the pay really, the boys are having their pocket money on Saturday for the pictures or anything they want.
I buy something little every week, we are having proper meals, no fry ups, so I can get something.
I want to get Ben some new shoes for school as the pair he has are hanging off his feet, he is coming home quite clean from school now, no paint or glue on his clothes, thank goodness.
Jane gave me two glass decanters (for holding drinks), hint, a lace set for the sideboard and two plants for I am going to send on any mail that comes for her.

Well Darling that's all my news for now. You will have to write like blazes to answer all the letters I have sent to you.

As soon as I get your letters I will write, I can't understand it, you will probably get them all at once, I hope I put the proper address.

Big hugs and kisses to our Daddy from your boys. I love you so much Darling and long to see you again soon. Take care of yourself, I miss you. All my love, write soon.
Your loving Wife and sons.
XXXXXXXXXXXXXXXX

Saturday Night 20 Sept
Dearest Darling,

Well I haven't heard from you for three days so I haven't a lot of news for you. I was up at seven o'clock this morning as it was picture day today, so I got them washed and dressed and walked down with them to the pictures. They were getting all upset because the crowd was small, they thought the picture had started, so they were all panic stations. I went round the town and did my week-end shopping and had a look round the shop windows (no spending) just looking.

Little Ed, David and myself went and had a cup of tea until the boys came out of the pictures, then we came home and had some dinner. The boys went out to play. I did some housework and some washing, then it was tea time.

I was going to do some ironing tonight but I am unwell and my legs and back were aching, so I will just leave it until tomorrow.

Alex and Ben had a nightmare last night, they woke up crying and screaming as Sarah's dog 'Titch' was killed at the bus stop yesterday morning right in front of them, they can't get over it, it must have been a terrible thing to happen , they are too young to understand.

The budgie is getting on well, he will sit on my finger, he did two rounds of the sitting room and flew up onto the pelmet. I couldn't flaming get him down. Betty laid an egg yesterday, but the baby threw it out, so I have to keep him away from the nesting box.

I can see 'Buddy' being a right soft bird, he lets me kiss and stroke him, he is a beautiful bird, he feeds himself now he looks a strong little bird, he jumps straight up into the nesting box.

I hope I get a letter from you on Monday.

Jane has gone home this morning, so I am lost, still I can please myself what I do. The boys are really missing you now, so am I, my Darling. I am longing to see you again, it seems to be ages since I saw you last. I love you so much. Take care of yourself, as I worry so much when I don't hear from you for a while.

Well that's all for now. I will leave this letter and give you my news tomorrow.

Goodnight my darling. I love you so much, God Bless, Take care. Love and kisses from us all.

Sunday 21 Sept

Well darling I will finish this letter to you now. I had a long lie until ten this morning, then I got their breakfast ready. The boys played out until twelve thirty then I gave them their dinner and they got washed and dressed for Sunday School, so after they had gone I took David and Little Ed down to the 'Green Shack' for a walk. I saw Mary Farmer and she asked me up for a coffee, so I went as I was really fed up today.

My neck and shoulders and back have been really painful the last few days, it could be because it has been cold and damp all of the last week. I will be going down to the town tomorrow so I will make an appointment to see the Doctor.

It has been raining most of today and the panel of wood on the fence it has been banging about all day, there is a strong wind and it is almost hanging off. I will see them again about fixing it.

The baby budgie is flying quite well now, when I shout 'Buddy' he looks down, he sits on my finger quite the thing, he has been cheeping his head off all day.

It will be three weeks on Wednesday since you left, it seems ages, I am getting fed up of my own company now. I have two pairs of shoes to buy tomorrow, it's too wet now for them wearing sandals.

Well my Darling that's all my news for now. Take good care of yourself.
I love you so much. I wish you were at home, I am lonely without you. Be good. Your boys are missing you, they keep asking if it's time for you to come home, still not long now. Bye for now.
Write to me soon Darling.

All our love is yours,
XXXXXXXXXXXXXXX

Wednesday 24

Dearest Darling,

Sorry about the paper but I have
run out and I wanted to write to you tonight as I
have been bad again with my back and if I didn't
write to you, you won't be having any letters.

I will answer your first letter now.
Yes! I got a nice long letter from Mary, she said it
looks although she is going to enjoy living out in
Bahrain, it shows you after all the fuss.
No! I haven't heard from the Beans again.
I have told you in all my letters about the bird, he
feeds himself, he flies round the room and the other
day I answered the door and he flew onto the front
door, I nearly had a fit, I pushed him back and
caught my perishing hand in the door.

I took Charlie to the Out Patients down at the
Hospital, they took the plaster off and there is still a
horrible gash, not big, but nasty looking, it hasn't
knitted together so he has to keep the plaster on a
week more, so I hope it's alright then.

The boys are all fretting in different ways, I'll be glad when you are home.

The Estate Repair Team have taken the fence over the back of us down and Vera and Mrs McNeils so when I asked , they said "I wasn't on the list", so I said "It was a disgrace to do all the rest when ours was falling to pieces", they said "It's too bad, you have to wait your turn". I have asked a few times and get the same answer every time.
The boys behave themselves at the pictures, but they are not going on Saturday as they were missing for two hours the other night, so for punishment they haven't been allowed to play out all this week, and no pictures.

I am trying to tame Buddy but I can't work miracles, it takes ages to tame them properly. Buddy has got some tail feathers quite long, but not long as long as Betty, Bobby or Jolly yet. No! He isn't grey, he is a lovely blue and violet.
You please yourself about more birds, these four make a devil of a mess already.
Yes! I got your reply letters to Wigfalls, I have enclosed another one I got the other day.

Monday I went down town and bought Ben and Charlie new shoes. Alex, Little Ed and David need some now, so I'll have to get a pair at a time as I have made myself short this week with paying out too much at a time.

My sister still hasn't had her baby, she is about ten days overdue, she won't be coming to keep me company when she has the baby, if she doesn't hurry up, it won't be worth her coming as it's not very long until you come back. It seems a long time seven weeks yet still we'll get through it as usual.

I had a letter from Jane, she got home safely and has herself a part-time job, she gets five Guineas a week, so it's a bit of money saved for Xmas.

I hope we can have a night out when you come home, I am sick of seeing these four walls, I have stopped having people in afternoons as I am sat every night on my own, still if I feel like working I can, or go to bed early if I like. I keep sleeping in as I have some different tablets for my back and they make me very sleepy, but the boys are always on time for school so far.

They are going to write to you at the weekend, okay.

Well that's all my news again, so Bye for now.

Take care darling, I love you and adore you. Be good.
We love you very much. God Bless. Write soon.

All my love, your loving Wife and sons
XXXXXXXXXXXXXXXXX

Thursday Night 25 Sept
Dearest Darling,

I haven't much news today, I had to go to see the Doctor today, he said if I am no better in a few weeks time, I have to go back and he is going to send me to the Hospital for Physiotherapy and I will probably have to have a special corset made, as the trouble I am having is gradually getting worse, and he said it's the start of a slipped disc. If I don't slow up a bit I will land up in bed for a while, I have to do as little as possible, which is hopeless in my case. You will have to bath the boys and do all the ironing and all the other things I can't do, when you come home. I am sorry love but that's the Doctor's orders.

I know you hate it when I am ill but it's better than me laid up in Hospital for months.

I came home tonight with terrible pain, so I took a couple of tablets, I am feeling all dopey as you can see by the writing. I have a standing order for tablets now, I just go to the Surgery and I get the prescription. It might get better, but he said it was hopeless trying to fool me, I am stuck with this back trouble, it might get better but he doesn't think so.

I hope you feel better than I do.

I got a letter from my Dad, there has been a lot of funny goings on and he said his girlfriend took some of his good clothes out of his wardrobe and pawned them. What a bitch! She needn't think she is going to give him a breakdown, or I'll be up there and sort her out, I can't just keep quiet and let her ruin his life, it's not fair.

The boys are asking for you and we miss you so much.
I will close now as I don't feel too good.
Take good care of yourself, I love you so much, God Bless.
Write soon darling, all my love is yours.
Love and kisses to Daddy from your boys
XXXXXXXXXXXXXXXXXXX

Wednesday Night 1 Oct

Dearest Darling,

Sorry I have been so long in writing but I haven't felt very well but I'll make up for it. The weather here is very cold and we have been having gale force winds.

The grass is growing fine but it's a good job that they didn't take our fence down, as they just trample all the grass down.

The boys are not allowed out to play anymore as I was told the other night that these two women were stood at the bus stop talking about me and they said "She shouldn't be allowed to keep them as she neglects them and lets them run wild". So to please everyone they stay in unless I take them out. I can't even let them play out now, still if they stay in it will stop them getting blamed for things they didn't do.

I phoned my Dad the other night and the first thing he said was "Auntie died Friday morning at one o'clock, didn't you get the telegram?" Everyone was there at the funeral. My Dad was very upset and I had a lot of trouble sleeping that night. I have been upset since I heard, especially as I didn't even get the telegram.

My sister still hadn't had her baby Monday night, but Dad said "She promised to come to make the arrangements about coming down and she hadn't turned up". So I have a feeling she must have started, My Dad said he might come for the night, if her husband hires a car, and it would be company for him when he travels back.
Hope you are well. It is four weeks tonight you have been away, six more, I hope it goes past quickly.

I will answer Friday's letter now.
I like the sound of the birds you have bought me, it will be a lovely collection.
I got myself three five shilling carpet pieces, it brightens the place up a bit.
I have also moved the green carpet into the sitting room and the grey carpet into the play room, it's a lot better and there isn't so much floor to scrub.
Little Ed will like the Mickey Mouse. David and Charlie would like a car, Alex a book and Ben doesn't know.

I hope your boss doesn't think he is putting you off about transferring, this place is getting me down.
Ann over the back husband Graham went to Bahrain for nine months today and the other Regiment come home tomorrow, I wish it was you

41

that was coming home tomorrow, I am fed up and lonely.

Sorry about the paper but I will get a new writing pad when I get my Family Allowance.

Could you send me some money to help to buy David, Ed and Alex some new shoes.

The Birth pills are no good for my back, I have got tablets. I have bought the two troughs for the cage.

Yes, Buddy broke the egg when he threw it out, but it must have been the last one for the year, as she hasn't laid anymore.

I am managing the Agencies alright, I got another query but I forgot to put it in the last letter, I will enclose in this one, if I remember.

Oh! Mrs McNeill has handed over the quarter, so she is going to send me her new address when she gets a Quarter in Germany, so then I'll send the slip back for her Agency, she is going to send the rest of her money each week.

Well that's all my news, Take care of yourself.

I Love you dearly, God Bless, write soon.

Your ever loving wife and sons, we miss you Darling

XXXXXXXXXXXXXXXXXXX

Thursday Night 2 Oct

Dearest Darling,

Well I didn't have a letter from you today, so I haven't much news.

It is very cold here and is dark by seven o'clock now. The boys are missing you and Little Ed keeps shouting "Come on Daddy", he is a scream, he looks into the envelope and says "Daddy's in there", some hope. The boys have ten days holiday off school from the 17th to 27th. I will have to find them some jobs to do. Last week they cleaned all the cupboards and drawers out in the kitchen, which was a big help. They will be going to the pictures this Saturday if they behave themselves.

Buddy has just flown onto my head and has been biting my ear to pieces, he kisses himself in the mirror and my arm aches as he loves himself and won't come away, he is running all over the writing pad and I have to manoeuvre the pen in between his tail. Ha! He is getting lovely and big now.

My sister still hasn't had the baby when Dad wrote last Tuesday, she can't be much longer.

I haven't heard about your sister, they never write so how am I supposed to know, I haven't her phone number or I could find out for you, seeing as you are desperate to know. I'll let you know if they write, remember your Mum and Dad must be on holiday by now. I might get a card shortly.

I will answer the letter I got from you yesterday. You won't be wanting eggs to eat when you come home, I'll make sure you have a nice meal when you come home. I hope you are not too energetic when you come home Ha! Ha! Ha!
No! Wigfalls haven't replied to your letters yet, I'll let you know when they do.

You had better not have a moustache, I hate them! No! David and Ed know now you are in Germany, so they don't even go to the corner which is best or they would be there all day.
Alex and Ben go to school with no bother unless the Benson and Taylor kids gang up on them and then they come home crying.
The boys are in bed by eight o'clock and sleep right through except when I get them up for the toilet before I go to bed.
This flaming baby bird is sat on my head scratching and flapping like mad, he has just walked all over your letter, so if you find a little souvenir from him,

don't be surprised. He is trying to catch the pen, as I am trying to write without covering his beak with ink, he won't let me write, his tail keeps getting in the way.

I do love you Darling, take good care of yourself. Write soon, be good Darling. God Bless.
I am looking forward to see you soon, six weeks today, it's lessening slowly but surely.

Your ever loving and devoted Wife and sons.
XXXXXXXXXXXXX

PS. The goldfish died yesterday, I don't know why?

Friday night 3 Nov
Dearest Darling,

Received your welcome letter and pleased to hear from you.

Well, my sister has finally had the baby, she has a baby girl, born Wednesday morning weighing in at 7lb 9oz, she said the baby is the image of her little sister. They are both well, but they would have liked another boy, but as she said you don't always get what you want in life, it's true. She hasn't given a date yet but she said a week or two.

In her Will Auntie left all her furniture to my Dad. He put a wreath on for us as everyone had gone to the funeral, and it would have looked bad if we had forgotten. I told Dad I would send him some money to cover the cost, as he can't afford to pay for us.

Captain Charles came down to see how I was getting on, he said he was going to Germany next week. He also said "It's your husband who has asked for a transfer?", so I said Yes! He said "You should have had an interview by now, but there wasn't anybody over there or something, but he was trying to arrange something for you. I told him I hadn't told you about all the trouble I am having, but he said just to

46

ignore it, people always gossip more so when the men are away.

I will answer your letter now, Charlie's head has healed up now and he is fighting fit again.
I am always glad when it's pay day, I have a little piece of liver or a chop once the boys are in bed.
Oh well, please yourself if you want another pair of birds (feathered kind I hope) if you want. If I say No! you still please yourself, so it's pointless asking isn't it.
The tablets are not bad, but make me so sleepy, I keep just waking up in time for the boy's school, I polish their shoes and lay their clothes out every night before I go to bed.
You don't want me to be laid up in bed, yet you won't help unless I keep on at you, that's why I just do a job myself, as you take so long to make up your mind to do it.

We miss you so much, I long to see you again, I am lonely without you my Darling, Five weeks on Wednesday.

You are a bossy boots aren't you? Cheerio for now, write soon, take care of yourself and be good.

I miss you and I love you with all my heart, God Bless.

Your ever loving Wife and sons
XXXXXXXXXXXXXXXXXXXX

Sat 18 Oct

Dearest Darling,

Sorry I have been so long in writing but I have not been very well. I have had a lot of cramp, but it's not too bad now.

It has not been very good weather here, very misty, cold and damp.

Well, my sister hasn't turned up, I wrote her two times last week but she hasn't answered them. Dad said she might be coming next week-end (which was yesterday) but never turned up, so it will probably be next week-end, which is rather late unless she stays only two weeks, as we want to be on our own when you come home don't we. It's dark here at half past six so the boys go to bed early.

Will you have any time off when you get home?

Alex has a Guinea Pig now, so he needs a cage made when you come home, it's name is Blackie and it's eleven weeks old, it gives me the creeps, but he loves it and speaks away to him as soon as he comes home, he goes straight to the box for him.

The birds are fine and we have three new goldfish, the boys are off school for ten days so I am not going down Ripon today, I am going to tidy up and take them for a walk down the river, it's not a very nice day, but what a noise they are making.

Mrs Kay wrote and told me she is going to pay the rest of the account herself, so I will write Wigfalls and send the slip for her Agency back to them.

I think if you look at the calendar the time passes more slowly, it is the eighteenth already, only three weeks, I hope it goes quickly. I have missed you very much Darling, I am longing to see you again, not very long now.

I thought you said you might get posted to Singapore. I don't fancy just staying at Colchester, still we'll see, you might know more when you have been to the interview. Did you see Capt Charles?

The boys were pleased when I told them of the presents. What do you mean I must behave myself, what have I done wrong?

We all feel better now, we had sore throats and earache last week, but we have recovered now.

There has been prowlers around here for the last two weeks and one woman was attacked. So once it's dark, I don't go outside the door and I close all the windows and draw the curtains. I won't even answer the door as that is their trick, they knock and scrape on the door and shout through the letter box. If anyone tries that I'll throw a bucket of water out the bathroom window, that will soon cool their ardour.

Are you not bringing any Rum this year? I could send you a £1 to get some if you want.
The overall you bought me sounds nice, it will keep me nice and smart for you my Darling. I have a nice grey dress and red shoes, so I will wear them the day you come home and look all smart.
My back isn't any better, I will probably go and see the Doctor before you come home, he said there's nothing more he can do except send me for physiotherapy and rest all I can, which is impossible.

We are missing you very much, I am frozen in bed every night, I am going to put my very cold feet all over yours Ha! Ha!
I got your love letter, I was beetroot when I read it, I can't write to you like that, there's a lot I would like to tell you, but I can't.

Little Ed is still looking for you in the envelope every day.

I don't bother with anyone, they are even blaming the boys for things when they haven't even been outside the door for six weeks, so what am I supposed to do. There is a load of kids always on the trailer and Alan's van, so when I chase them they just laugh at me and go straight back on there again. That bloody cat sits there all the time, you should see the state of the canvas, well I can't do anymore, I have done all I can.

You say send Charlie to sort them out, well that German woman said she will give them a good hiding if they throw stones, yet it's the other kids are doing it, but it's ours who get the blame for it.

Oh! By the way, The Doctor suggests no sex for one year, that will make my back better. Ha! Ha! What will you do now? I'll give you some of my tablets, so we'll both be sleepy together. Okay. Ha! Ha!

Well Darling that's all my news for now. Take care of yourself. We miss you so much and I love you dearly.

God Bless. See you soon. Write soon.

Your ever loving Wife and sons.

XXXXXXXXXXXXXXXXX

PS. I haven't heard from your Mum and Dad.

Monday Morning 20 Oct
Dearest Darling,

Well I received your two letters this
morning, look it's no use sending nasty letters to me,
I have explained in my last letter to you I can't help
it if they got mislaid. I posted them, so stop thinking
I am getting at you by not writing.

I'll answer your first letter now. I suppose I'll be
getting these letters until you receive mine
explaining, I felt a right fool saying to Captain
Charles," I have written to him, as for people talking
behind your back, well they can talk".
That's your trouble, if you don't hear every day you
think Oh! she must be up to something, some
chance, with the boys here round me all day.
I gave your boys your love and kisses.

Now for letter No 2.
Why must you always think I am taking my spite
out on you, if you don't get a letter.
What do you expect me to do, write to all the
workshops explaining why you haven't had a letter
for a week, well I won't and if you don't write a
decent letter I won't bother to answer them.

You act like a big kid sometimes. That's bloody good, I never shown any interest in the car, that's' how I got £50 for a new engine, how many times have I said go and do your car, so don't say I am not interested.

If that's how they are treating you at the workshop just let them get on with it, don't worry yourself about them, you know we all love you here at home, even if you feel no-one cares, it's not true.

Well that's all the answers to your two letters.

I will give you my news now.

Nothing much changes here, the weather is still the same, cold and damp.

The fence is still the same, I am glad they didn't take our one down now as they have been down for seven weeks, and they have no woods to repair them, and that's the ones the prowler has been to.

We are all not too bad now, although we still have the cold. I am so sore and stiff, I feel as though somebody has hit me across the back with a stick, still I just have to put up with it, if you only knew the pain every time I move, maybe you would be more sympathetic, still I have my tablets and if you keep sending nasty letters I will dope myself up, so I will be snoozy when you come home and you know once I am asleep that's it. So then that will fix you Ha! Ha! Only joking love!

For goodness sake Darling only eighteen days left, we'll soon be together again, till then remember I do love you very much. Take care of yourself. See you soon. We miss you and need you.
Your ever loving Faithful Wife and sons.
XXXXXXXXXXXXXXXXXXXXXXXXXXXX

Wednesday 22 Oct

Dearest Darling,

Well I haven't much news for you until I get another letter from you.

Captain Charles came down and asked why I hadn't written to you? Well I know I didn't write last week as I told you. I wasn't very well with cramp in my hands, I couldn't even tie the boy's shoes or wring the washing out. Oh! The spin dryer has gone again. I have written at least three times a week except last week, so I don't know what has happened to the ones I wrote, I knew you would be worried when I didn't write.

We went for a walk to the river this afternoon, and then after tea I phoned my Dad, he said my sister has said that she wasn't coming down, so I said to Dad, to tell her to write and tell me definitely. I won't ask her again that's for sure.

I am so lonely I could even put up with her company, that's how desperate I am for a bit of company. Still I keep thinking my Darling will soon be home, that's all I think of these days. When I will see you again, it will be funny to sleep in the same bed again Ha! Ha!

will put Alex's letter in with this one, they are really fed up now. "How many days left now Mum?"

I will answer your letters as soon as I receive them, sorry about the letters, but my fingers were so sore and stiff and my legs and toes, it's so damp these days.
Take good care of yourself, we love you so much and long to see you again soon, only nineteen days thank goodness.

Well my Darling that's all my news for now.
I love you Darling, God Bless. Write soon.
Your loving Wife and sons
XXXXXXXXXXXXXXXXXXX

Saturday 25 October

Dearest Darling,

Well I didn't have a letter today, I am surprised you are still waiting to hear from Capt Charles, as he said he would send the signal straight back saying I had been writing, so I don't know what's happened. Every letter I get there hasn't been a kind word for me, it's really upset me, when you have sent your love to the boys and not to me. I have dreaded every letter from you, but by now you should have got at least one letter from me. I have quite a lot of cramps in my hands this past week and wringing out the clothes hasn't helped any.

The boys didn't go to the pictures this morning as I was short of money, so we had a lie in, and just cleared up the rest of today. The boys stayed up until eleven o'clock tonight to keep me company, so they have just trotted upstairs to bed. They go back to school Monday, thank goodness, what a week. I never finished cleaning all the time they were home. It's getting really cold here, in fact the boys don't want to play out because it's so cold.

I miss you so much, not long now darling, only two weeks. Don't be angry at me, you can hardly say I haven't written enough since you've been away can you? Hope you received my letters okay? Also Alex's letter, his spelling was terrible, but he got all upset when I kept correcting him, so I just let him send it.

There was a terrible thunderstorm the night before last and the fence kept banging the whole night long and I kept waking up. Last night I locked the gate and this morning it was wide open, so there must have been someone creeping around. It's terrible when you can't even go outside the door when it's dark in case you get attacked. Well I haven't much news so I will close now, but will write a short letter to you tomorrow.

Bye for now. Take care don't worry Darling. I love you and miss so much, God Bless, Your ever loving and faithful Wife. Love and kisses to Daddy from your Boys.
Is it the eleventh or twelfth you come home?
XXXXXXXXXXXXXXX

Sunday 26ᵗʰ October
Dearest Darling,

Just a short letter for you, I haven't
any news as I wrote you last night, but I will write
so you know I am still here and not run off
somewhere, as you seem to think every time you
don't get a letter, still I am not resorting to sarcasm as
it is very hurtful and I have had enough this week.
Well I have the bedrooms, ironing and the clothes to
get ready for tomorrow as they are back to school. I
am phoning to see when Charlie can start school or
put his name on the list. I will see if David can go to
kindergarten.

The boys say they miss you and we are all looking
forward to see you soon.
I never got my lie in this morning just because the
sun was shining, they were up like larks, still, they
will be in bed early tonight, as they have to be up
early in the morning.

I hope you have heard from me by now, I can't write
every day as I only buy stamps on a Monday. I can
never afford to buy any through the week.

Well, that's it again nothing very interesting.
Let me know what date you will be here or haven't you had your date yet?

We miss and love you very much, take care. God Bless.
All our love is yours.
Your Loving Wife and sons
XXXXXXXXXXXXXXXXXXX

PS. Guinea Pig 1   Budgies 4   Goldfish 3

Ha! Ha!

Sunday Night 26th October
Dearest Darling,
                    Just a short letter to show I haven't
forgotten you.
I haven't a lot of news as I wrote you two letters this
week-end already.
I did the bedrooms this afternoon and as it was nice
and sunny I let the boys out to play today, they look
pale and were fed up of staying in, they were no
bother and I told them if the other kids gang up on
them for the lot of them to fight like hell against
them, still I can't keep them indoors to please
neighbours.
I counted all my cigarette coupons and have two
small surprises coming for you from the Cigarette
Catalogue, they are not very big, but something
useful. I also have a small present for you from the
boys' which is upstairs in your drawer. I hope you
like them.

Well it's late again and I am tired, the boys are back
to school again and I have to be up early and make
sure they get off alright. I have to go down town
shopping.

We miss you and are looking forward to see you soon. Not long my darling. Take good care of yourself. I love you.

Bye for now. God Bless.
Your loving Wife and sons.
XXXXXXXXXXXXXXXXXXXXXXXXXXXX

Tuesday 28th October

Dearest Darling,

Received your welcome letter yesterday and so pleased to get a nice letter from you. I got the £5, I will get them their shoes as soon as possible.

I will give you my news first, then I will answer your letter my Darling.

Monday I went down shopping, I gave the boys their dinner down town, then we took our time looking round the shops and had a slow walk home. I met Vicky so she asked me in for a coffee, so I went and I got back home at four then. I cleaned up, made the tea, got the boys ready for bed, then I did some washing and ironing for the day. I cleaned the sitting room and washed the net curtains, then, I made the dinner and did washing in the afternoon. I have loads of ironing, so I stood all evening and got it all finished.

I changed all the beds and have been washing all morning, I think I have done the most of it now. Now I have a stack of ironing to do tonight.

I got a letter from Jane, she is coming back on Saturday.

The boys keep asking "How many more days yet?"

It's Bonfire night next Wednesday, I will probably take them over to the bonfire, I will get them a few fireworks, I suppose only sparklers, and coloured fountains, no bangers or jumping ones, they are too dangerous.

As you can see by my writing my hands are bothering me again, I have an appointment with Dr Jones tomorrow afternoon, so I'll let you know how I get on.

The birds are fine, I have Buddy in the bottom cage, Jolly in the other, and baby and Betty in the top cage. I think Betty is 'preggers' again, it's not my fault. All the birds keep fighting Buddy, so I had to put him on his own.

The grass is not too bad, it needs cutting again, I have done it twice since you went to Germany.

Little Ed is a right little talker now, he says "Pardon me Mummy", "I'm telling Mummy   David", "Daddy is in the Germany on scheme", and he laughs like anything.

Well that's all my news so I'll answer your letter now.

I'm sorry you were worried, I hope you are alright now. Captain Charles took long enough didn't he. He came and saw me on the Monday, he should have let you know before Friday.
I didn't say I couldn't use my hands, I said I keep getting cramp, that's what I am going about tomorrow to the Doctors.

You dare grow a moustache!

Dr Jones said a heat lamp would help my back, still we'll see, I haven't got anything for Xmas yet.
I just wonder if you have any time off? It would be nice to spend some time with you. I didn't mean anything.

Well Darling that's all my news for now. I will write tomorrow, I hope I get a letter from you and then I can write a longish letter.

Look after yourself, not long now darling. We miss you very much and are looking forward to see you soon.
Cheerio for now, God Bless, Your ever Loving and Faithful Wife and sons.
XXXXXXXXXXXXXXXXX

Tuesday 4th November
Dearest Darling,
                    Received your welcome letters, I
didn't realise that tomorrow was the last day I could
send letters. Why are you not home on Monday like
the rest?
Looking forward to seeing you in eight days time
thank goodness, we are hoping the last few days pass
quickly.
I got Alex a pair of Tuf shoes and Little Ed some
brown Clarke's shoes, I didn't have quite enough, so I
will get David some next Monday.
I have been frozen the last few days, I'll be glad
when you come home so I can put my freezing feet
on yours, Ha! Ha!

We stayed down town yesterday until four o'clock, so
it passed nicely.
The fish and chip shop opened up at the building
site last night, I was dying to go, but was too scared
to go out in case we got attacked, still there is plenty
of time.
I have been cleaning and doing the sheets today, so I
will do my ironing tonight.

It is freezing here and some parts of Yorkshire had snow yesterday, its cold enough for snow.

I still haven't had a letter from my sister, I don't know what I have done but she was saying she was looking forward to see us all, and she doesn't even write now.

Jane came back Saturday, I did a lot of back and forth posting mail to her and her mail is still coming here, she promised she would bring me an ornament, but she hasn't said anything.

Little Ed threw a car up and knocked the lampshade down in the play-room, so that will cost a bit to replace.

I have some Avon cosmetics coming, so could you lend me £3 to pay them when you come home and I will pay you back when I can.

Betty has laid another egg, her and Bobby have been giving it rice, as Alex said the other day "Mum look, Betty likes a piggy back" He! He! They are at it nearly every night, so we might have more than one this time. I hope so.

I have to go to the Doctor on Thursday, as he couldn't find the results of the X-ray, so he's not

sure what he is treating. My hands and feet are not good but we are managing not too bad. I keep dropping things 'especially plates'. Oops!
I have a lovely bruise where I had the blood test.
Well the boys are going to the bonfire tomorrow night, only for an hour, as it very cold, especially for the little ones.

I keep saying "Daddy's coming next week" to the boys and Little Ed says "Not, Not".
You will see the difference, he is a proper little scallywag like the rest.
I have put the four of them in the big bedroom as Ben was on his own, and was always getting the cold, so they are top and tail all together. If they start messing about I will separate them, but if not, they are a lot warmer, as it is cold upstairs.
It is dark at six o'clock, I sometimes let them stay up until half past seven and they get to stay up until late Friday and Saturday and go to bed not later than seven on a Sunday.

I got the boys a five shilling box of showers and one rocket, no bangers and two packets of sparklers. So I will let them watch out the front as Len usually lights them all so there is no accidents.

Last week Ben came home with twelve cards for five shillings from school and I had to buy them, as he got upset when I said No!

It's one thing after another, I haven't let them to the pictures for about four weeks now, and they keep asking if they can go, still I'll probably let them go next Saturday when you are home.

Well that's all my news again Darling, I suppose this had better be my last letter to you as they wouldn't reach you in time, if I sent any more after tomorrow.

We miss and love you so much Darling, not long now, take care of yourself until we see you next week. God Bless. Safe journey.

Your ever Loving Wife and sons.
XXXXXXXXXXXXXXXXXX

Summary

Having read all of my Wife's letters of 1969 I feel upset, because back in 1969 this was 'the norm' of Service Life. All the emotions, and problems that Wife's and especially the children had to endure whilst their husbands and fathers were away for long periods.

For the Unit it was a 10 week period of training and exercises, this in itself brought long hours and stresses to everyone taking part.

This does not explain what some of my letters to my Wife contained during 1969, but what with 'mail' delivery delays during the exercise, to and from the Units, didn't help.

My Wife wrote it as it was, some of her letters to me were upsetting, especially about the problems that the boys were experiencing, and how it disturbed them emotionally. The fights, allegations and the bed wetting, even the wives' gossip didn't help. But even in Germany, there was gossip going around about the wives' and children, which didn't help matters.

Now nearly 50 years later, it saddens me that this all happened, it is unique to the Forces, and at that time there was little or no support for the families.

My Wife did a wonderful job with our children, managing in spite of all her ailments. She certainly was a devoted Wife and Caring Mother, I hope that reading her letters now that you will understand just how tough her life was at times. But she saw the family through, she was our 'rock' that we all relied upon. Bless her.

My memories of these times have long diminished, and I am glad that she managed to 'acquire and save' these letters, because it has reminded me of just what her, and the children's lives were like. And it saddens me deeply, especially now.
Through these letters I feel that my wife is still 'talking' to me, which I now find to be comforting.
Sadly, you never fully appreciate what you have, until it is 'lost' to you, forever.

Bilko
February 2020

Bilko has been writing since 2014 and a member of the Lincoln U3A Creative Writing Group, contributing to their anthology 'Creations'.

He has also written 'Bilko's Book of Banter', a collection of humorous poems, with a different view of life.

Printed in Poland
by Amazon Fulfillment
Poland Sp. z o.o., Wrocław

57102636R00043